Animal Safari Nature Library

Killer Whales and Dolphin Play

by Don Arthur Torgersen

Photographs by Lee Trail
and Don Torgersen

Consulting Editor
Gilbert K. Boese, Ph.D.
Director
Milwaukee County Zoo

 CHILDRENS PRESS, CHICAGO

Acknowledgments

The author would like to thank the following institutions for assistance given in the development of this series: Chicago Zoological Society and Brookfield Zoo, Lincoln Park Zoo, Field Museum of Natural History, Milwaukee County Zoo, Minnesota Zoological Garden, St. Louis Zoo, Denver Zoo, San Diego Zoo, West Palm Beach Zoo, Lion Country Safari, Miami Seaquarium, Crandon Park Zoological Gardens on Key Biscayne, Sea World, National Zoological Park in Washington, D.C., Worthley N.L. Burbank Nature Center.

Project Editor: Joan Downing

Library of Congress Cataloging in Publication Data

Torgersen, Don Arthur, 1934-
   Killer whales and dolphin play.
   (Animal safari nature library)
   Summary: Discusses the characteristics, behavior, and
habitats of marine mammals such as whales, dolphins, sea
lions, seals, and walruses.
   1. Marine mammals—Juvenile literature. [1. Marine
mammals. 2 Mammals] I. Trail, Lee, ill. II. Title. III.
Series: Torgersen, Don Arthur, 1934- Animal
safari nature library.
QL713.2.T67   599.5   81-15480
ISBN 0-516-00653-3   AACR2

1 2 3 4 5 6 7 8 9 10 11 12 R 89 88 87 86 85 84 83 82

Contents

Sea lions live on land as
well as in the sea. All
marine mammals must
breathe air to live.

Marine Mammals—Life in the Sea

On planet Earth, the first forms of plant and animal life appeared in the sea more than 600 million years ago. Today, the sea covers more than 70 percent of the earth's surface. It is teeming with plant and animal life and a wide variety of colorful *species.*

Many warm-blooded animals live in the sea. Whales, porpoises, dolphins, sea lions, seals, walruses, sea otters, and sea cows are *marine mammals.*

Fish and reptiles are cold-blooded animals. The body heat of a cold-blooded animal changes with that of the surrounding air or water. The body heat of a fish is about the same as the temperature of the water surrounding it. If the temperature changes, the fish's body heat changes.

The body heat of a marine mammal, like most large mammals, remains constant at about ninety-eight degrees Fahrenheit. If the water or outside temperature changes, a mammal's body heat still remains the same. That is why mammals are called warm-blooded animals. Only mammals and birds are warm-blooded animals.

Most fish lay eggs. But marine mammals give birth to live young. They nurse on their mothers' milk during the first year of their lives.

To survive, fish have gills through which sea water, rich in oxygen, passes. Marine mammals have lungs and must breathe air to restore oxygen and survive.

Sea cows are *herbivores,* or plant-eating animals. But all other marine mammals are *carnivores,* or meat-eating animals. They cannot survive by eating plant food. They prey on fish and other animals in the sea.

*The harbor seal is a
common marine
mammal with a beautiful
face.*

In the sea, as on land, all life depends on plant growth. Marine *algae* are tiny, microscopic plants that drift near the surface in saltwater seas. These tiny plants—or micro-algae—absorb and store energy from sunlight. Their growth depends not only on energy from sunlight but also on salt minerals that drain into the oceans from land. During daylight, marine algae produce oxygen, which is necessary for all life in the sea.

Plankton is all the tiny plant and animal life that drift with the currents near the sea's surface. *Zooplankton* are the tiny, swimming animals that drift in the sea. *Krill*, which are shrimplike animals, tiny crabs and snails, and small shellfish are zooplankton. Their tiny shells and hard body parts often wash up on sandy beaches. Jellyfish, water fleas, and billions of fish eggs and larvae also drift on the sea's surface.

6

The walrus is a comical marine mammal with a bearded face.

The zooplankton feed on micro-algae. They convert the plant matter into animal protein. In turn, zooplankton are fed on by larger sea animals and fishes.

Small fish are eaten by bigger fish. Zooplankton and fish are eaten by marine mammals. Some marine mammals are eaten by larger marine mammals. To be swallowed by another creature is the natural course for more than 90 percent of all sea animals.

Between 50 million and 100 million years ago, the ancestors of whales, dolphins, sea lions, walruses, and other marine mammals lived on land. But these early land animals began to swim and feed in shallow coastal waters. Before long, they became entirely adapted to an aquatic (water) way of life. Eventually, they moved farther into the seas and oceans. Today, most marine mammals live in the colder waters of the world's seas.

A beluga whale swims
slowly beneath the
surface of the water by
moving its broad tail
flukes up and down.

8

A Tale of Whales

In the cold Arctic Ocean between the ice floes, a huge female blue whale rises high in the water, rolls, and splashes down broadside. Great waves roll from each side of her body. She swims slowly toward a large swarm of krill. She cruises right into the swarm, opens her huge mouth until it is filled with krill and salty seawater, then closes it. The seawater strains out, and the blue whale swallows millions of krill in one gulp.

The blue whale is the largest animal that ever existed. But it feeds on some of the smallest creatures in the sea. One mouthful of krill provides the whale with a great deal of rich animal protein and vitamins.

Female blue whales are generally larger than the males. A large female may exceed one hundred feet in length and weigh more than 150 tons. Her weight is equal to that of twenty-five or thirty elephants. If her jawbone were stood up on land like a great arch, one of the large, extinct dinosaurs could walk underneath it.

There are ninety-two species of whales. Blue or finback whales, gray whales, sperm whales, humpback whales, and right whales are large-sized whales between thirty-five and one hundred feet in length. Killer whales and white or beluga whales are medium-sized whales between fifteen and thirty feet long. Dolphins and porpoises are the smallest whales. They are only five to fifteen feet in length.

Most whales live in herds in the colder parts of saltwater seas and oceans. The beluga or white whale, which lives in coastal waters and bays in the Arctic regions, often swims up the large Arctic rivers. Some dolphin species live in freshwater rivers and in a few lakes in South America and India. River dolphins live alone or in small groups.

An animal loses its body heat twenty-five times faster in water than in air. Whales have smooth-skinned bodies with no fur, except for a few hairs around the nose and the mouth. They have developed a layer of fatty blubber under the skin. The blubber insulates the whale's body and prevents heat loss.

Large whales have thicker blubber than small whales have. In the right whale, a large slow-swimming whale, the blubber is often twenty to twenty-five inches thick. Some fast-swimming large whales have blubber layers of only six to eight inches. Because they swim so fast, their bodies produce more heat. They don't need as much blubber to stay warm.

Like all mammals, if a whale overheats, it will die. It cannot live long outside of water. Whales stranded on beaches during low tides often become overheated. Heat stroke is the main cause of death for stranded whales.

Whales swallow their food without chewing it. Because they are in the sea, they normally take in a lot of salt with their food. If a mammal has too much or too little salt in its blood, it will die. Most land mammals give off salt through sweat glands. Whales do not have sweat glands. Instead, they have double-sized kidneys. Large amounts of salt pass out with the urine.

Most female whales have pregnancies of ten to twelve months. They give birth to a single calf that looks exactly like its parents. Most large mammals are born head first, but whales are born tail first. After birth, the mother pushes her calf to the surface so it can fill its lungs with air for the first time.

Whale calves nurse underwater. Whale milk is rich in fat and protein, and the calves grow very fast. During its first year, the blue whale calf gains about 220 pounds each day. It grows more than thirty feet in seven months.

*A beluga or white whale
is "spy hopping" to see
across the surface of the
water.*

A whale's broad tail fin is called the flukes. The tail flukes help to power the whale forward in swimming. Whales do not have hind limbs.

The whale's forelimbs are called flippers. They are used in steering and diving.

How Do Whales Swim?

Many large whales migrate thousands of miles each year. They breed in colder waters and calve (give birth) in warmer waters. Some herds cruise at speeds of fifteen to twenty miles an hour. A few of the smaller species swim twenty-five to thirty miles an hour.

A fish swims by moving its tail from side to side. A whale swims by moving its powerful tail up and down. The broad, horizontal tail *flukes* sweep up and down. Each beat of the tail helps to drive the whale foward. The *pectoral fins,* or *flippers,* steer the whale when it turns or dives.

Whales dive very deep. Blue whales normally dive 25 to 100 feet, but sometimes reach depths of more than 1,000 feet. They stay underwater for four to forty minutes before coming up for air. Sperm whales can dive 2,000 feet or more and can stay underwater for fifty to ninety minutes. Dolphins and porpoises dive 75 to 100 feet, but sometimes reach depths of 250 feet.

Like all mammals, whales must breathe free oxygen to live. But they do not have to exchange air as often as land mammals do. A man breathes about sixteen times per minute, but a dolphin breathes only one to three times per minute. Many land mammals carry about 35 percent oxygen in their lungs, 12 percent in muscles, 41 percent in blood, and 12 percent in other body tissues. A whale carries only 9 percent oxygen in its lungs, but 41 percent in its muscles, 41 percent in its blood, and 9 percent in its remaining body tissues. The oxygen must be replenished regularly. Otherwise the muscles, brain, and other body tissues will die.

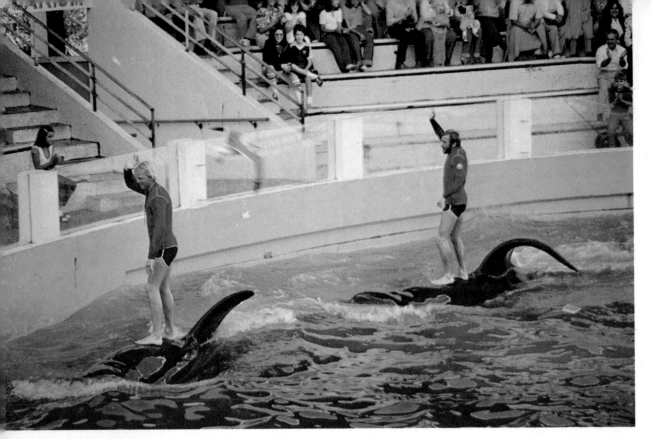

Trainers enjoy a ride on two killer whales.

Whales breathe through their nostrils or *blowhole.* The blowhole is on the highest point of the head. After a dive, the whale must return to the surface to take a new breath of air. It expels moist air from its lungs with a great blast through its blowhole. In large whales, this white cloud of steam rises fifteen to twenty-five feet above the whale's head. In the nineteenth century, when a whale hunter spotted the white blast from his ship, he yelled, "Thar she blows!"

Some scientists in the nineteenth century believed that whales could not make voice sounds. But whale hunters and sailors knew all along that whales made moaning, mewing, creaking, whooping, screaming, squealing, and clicking sounds. They also knew that whales had a remarkable sense of hearing.

Many large whales live for thirty to forty years.

Large whales have provided many useful products. Oil taken from the blubber once was used to keep oil lamps burning. Oil also comes from the bones. Today, whale oil is used mainly in margarine and soaps. It also is used to make high-quality candle wax and to lubricate precision machinery and instruments. People in Japan and Western Europe as well as Eskimos and Indians eat whale meat. The meat also is processed into pet food, cattle feed, and poultry feed. Whale bones are crushed and used to make glue, gelatin, and fertilizers. Tough tissue fibers are used as strings on tennis rackets. Ivory jawbones are used as tools and in handcrafts.

Blue whales, right whales, and other large species have been hunted nearly to extinction. The herds must be free to breed and reproduce in fair numbers. Otherwise many of these great swimming mammals will disappear forever from our oceans and seas.

A whale breathes through its nostrils or blowhole. In dolphins and other toothed whales, the blowhole is a single opening.

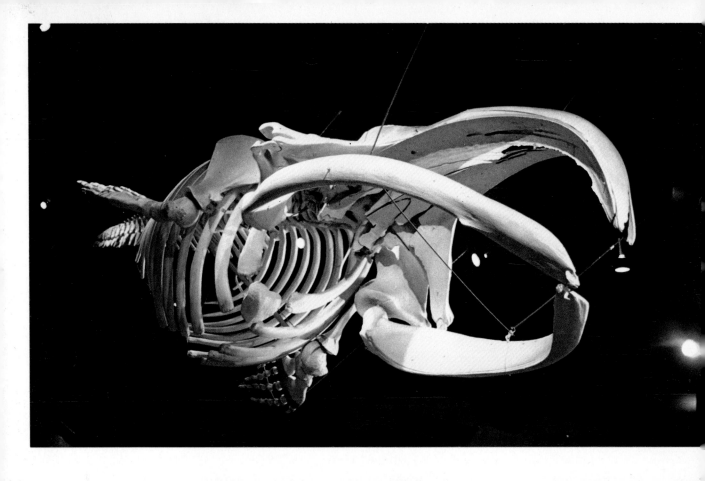

The skeleton of a toothed whale. These whales have peglike teeth.

16

The skeleton and jawbone of a fifty-foot baleen whale. All giant whales, except the sperm whale, are baleen whales and do not have teeth.

Baleen Whales

Biologists classify all whales as *cetaceans*. The ninety-two species are grouped into two orders—*baleen whales* and *toothed whales.*

Most large whales are baleen whales. The sperm whale, which grows to sixty-five feet, is the only large, toothed whale.

Baleen whales have two nostrils, or a double blowhole, on the top of the head. The nostrils are not fused into a single opening or blowhole.

Baleen whales do not have teeth. Instead, their mouths are equipped with a row of baleen plates. These are used to strain tiny zooplankton from the sea. The baleen are long, horny plates that hang down side by side from the roof of the whale's mouth. These horny plates are often called *whalebone.*

When feeding on swarms of krill or on schools of tiny fish, the baleen whale also draws enormous quantities of sea water into its mouth. The whale's tongue presses against the gums when the mouth is closed. This forces the water out through the baleen plates. The tiny sea animals are then swallowed whole.

Blue whales, rorqual whales, sei whales, gray whales, humpback whales, and right whales are among the large baleen whale species.

Dolphins and killer whales are toothed whales. The teeth are suited for grabbing and holding prey before swallowing it.

Toothed Whales

Killer whales, dolphins, porpoises, and pilot whales are grouped in a family called *delphinids*, or dolphinlike animals. These whales are toothed whales. Nearly all toothed whales, except the sperm whale, are small or medium-sized.

The nostrils of toothed whales are fused to form a single blowhole, used for breathing. Toothed whales have no sense of smell. They rely entirely on eyesight and sound to find food.

The hind limbs are totally missing. As with all whales, the tail and tail flukes provide the power of locomotion.

In toothed whales, the peglike or conelike teeth are uniform in size and shape. The teeth are not specialized into incisors, canines, and molars as are the teeth of land mammals. The whale can grab prey, such as fish and squid, with its teeth. But the teeth cannot chew. The food is swallowed whole. When toothed whales lose their teeth, they do not lose the ability to catch and swallow food.

The bottle-nosed dolphin has 80 to 104 teeth. Some smaller dolphin species have 200 to 260 teeth. Killer whales have 40 to 56 teeth. The beluga whale has 32 to 40 teeth. The narwhal has only two teeth. In the male narwhal, one of the teeth develops into a long, spiral tusk.

19

A killer whale responds
to pats, scratches, rubs,
and the words of its
trainer.

Black-and-White Wolves of the Sea

In the ocean near Antarctica, a pack of killer whales is *spy hopping.* Several whales are hopping straight up in the water to get a good look across the surface. They hold the front part of their bodies out of the water for several seconds. They spot a large ice floe in the distance. A herd of sea lions is resting on it.

One of the killer whales slaps its flukes against the water and dives. The loud, splashing sound causes the other killer whales to dive and follow.

A few minutes later, loud, booming noises ring out at the ice floe. The sea lions are alarmed and begin to bark. The killer whales are battering the bottom of the ice floe with their heads.

Suddenly, the ice floe begins to shake and crack, breaking into several parts. Several of the sea lions dive off the ice and race toward the shore. Some of them are caught and quickly eaten by the killer whales.

Killer whales often hunt in packs made up of both sexes. They will probably eat anything that swims in the sea. Their main food source, however, is fish and squid. But they also eat octopus, sea lions, seals, and dolphins whenever they get the chance. On rare occasions, they may gorge themselves on the carcass of a dead baleen whale. They even eat its blubber and tongue.

Killer whales have distinct black-and-white markings. The sickle-shaped dorsal fin and the flippers are black all over.

Killer whales are swift, powerful swimmers and divers. They are found in the colder parts of all oceans around the world. They are the largest members of the dolphin family. Many large males grow twenty-five to thirty feet in length and weigh six to eight tons. The females are somewhat smaller.

Because they hunt in packs, killer whales have been called "wolves of the sea." The killer whale's smooth skin is black on the back and white on the undersides. There is a white oval patch just behind and above each eye. The forelimbs, or flippers, are black all over. The underside of the tail flukes is white. The killer whale has a long, black dorsal fin, which is triangular or sickle-shaped.

22

*Two killer whales leap
high out of the water,
following the signal of
their trainer.*

Orca is another name for the killer whale. When killer whales swim in packs, the females and the young are generally in the middle. The males are on the outside of the main group. Sometimes they stay separate from the group. A male leader often slaps his flukes against the water or leaps out of the water and splashes down broadside as a signal for the entire pack to move on.

Despite its reputation as a fearless predator in the sea, killer whales in captivity are easily tamed, trained, and made dependent on keepers. In marine parks, exhibitions, and shows, killer whales delight people with great leaps and splashes. Trainers swim with them or ride on their backs. They even put their heads into the large mouths of these toothed whales without fear or harm. Killer whales prove to be friendly, affectionate creatures.

*A dolphin leaps high
into the air and snatches
a fish right out of its
trainer's mouth.*

Playful Dolphins

Dolphins are the smallest whales, but they swim in the largest herds. Some herds, or schools, have three hundred or four hundred members. A few herds may have as many as a thousand dolphins.

Dolphins love to play. They follow ships at sea and ride on the bow waves. They spend hours leaping and diving over and over again, jumping straight up into the air, or dancing around on the water on their tail flukes. They throw fish back and forth to each other with their mouths as if they were playing catch with a ball.

The bottle-nosed dolphin is the playful whale that performs in dolphin shows. It is also commonly called a porpoise.

There are other species of toothed whales called common dolphins, common porpoises, finless black porpoises, and bottle-nosed whales. There are also two species of brightly colored fish called dolphin fish. One of them is as large as a small whale.

Bottle-nosed dolphins or "porpoises" are easy to catch. They swim in fairly shallow coastal waters. They are easy to tame and train, and they breed well in captivity.

Dolphins feed mainly on fish. They swim into large schools of fish and snap up one or two fish at a time with their toothed beaks. They swallow the fish whole. Dolphins also feed on squid, which rise from lower levels of the sea toward the surface during the night.

The bottle-nosed dolphin is a very intelligent and curious animal. It can perform many tricks, responding to voice and whistle signals and hand and arm movements from a trainer. Dolphins like to be touched, petted, and scratched. They like people to talk to them. Most of all, they like to eat the fish with which their trainers reward them after each trick. Perhaps this is why they always seem to have a grin on their faces.

When dolphins and killer whales are kept in large tanks and aquariums, crude salt is added to the water. This enables the animals to float more easily and helps prevent certain skin problems.

Hearing is the most important sense for all whales. Scientists have found that a dolphin's eyesight is as good as a man's above the surface of the water. But the dolphin's hearing range is four times greater than a cat's and ten times greater than a man's. A man can hear sounds up to 20,000 vibrations per second. A dolphin can hear sounds up to 200,000 vibrations per second.

Dolphins find schools of fish or squid, and other objects in the sea, by means of *echolocation*. They send out high-pitched clicking sounds from their foreheads. The sounds travel through the water, bounce off objects like an echo, and return to the whale's inner ears and brain. This is a form of sonar. It guides the whale directly to the object. A dolphin can find a golf ball on the bottom of the ocean through echolocation. Some scientists who study animal behavior think that dolphins can stun their prey with sound.

Dolphin trainers give their animals physical checkups twice a year. Divers enter the water and round up the dolphins one at a time. Once the dolphin is out of the water, its skin must be kept moist so the animal's body will not overheat.

Blood and urine samples are taken. Experts listen to the heartbeat. The animal's temperature is taken to make sure it is about ninety-eight degrees Fahrenheit. The dolphin is measured and weighed. Its blowhole is examined to make sure there are no parasites in the nostrils. After the examination, the dolphin is returned to the water.

In captivity, dolphins live for twenty-five to thirty years. A few have lived longer.

Dolphins like to have their tongues rubbed and scratched.

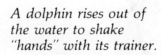

A dolphin rises out of the water to shake "hands" with its trainer.

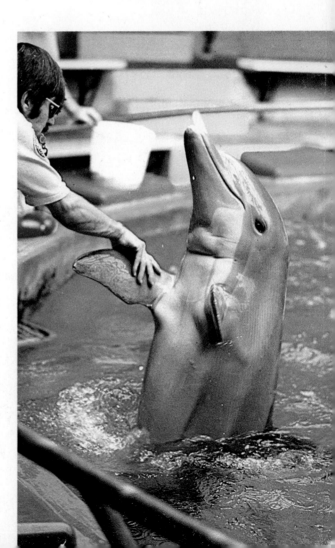

Dolphins develop strong bonds of affection with human beings.

A zoo dolphin's mouth, teeth, and blowhole are examined by a doctor. A healthy dolphin will live for twenty-five or thirty years.

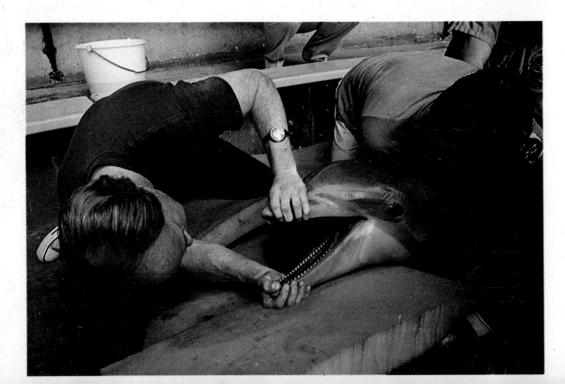

A dolphin advises his trainer about the hazards of smoking.

The seal humps and wriggles when moving on land. Its forelimbs provide little help.

The sea lion supports its weight on its flippers when moving on land.

Dolphins and whales do not go on land. They spend their entire lives in the water.

Sea Lions, Seals, and Walruses

On a rocky island off the coast of northern California, a herd of sea lions is basking in the sun. One large bull sits on a rock and begins to bark loudly. He is surrounded by a harem of twenty cows. Several of the females begin to join in the barking. Others roll on their backs and scratch their coats against the rocks.

In the North Atlantic, a beautiful, silver-furred seal pup sits alone on an ice floe. Nearby is a hole in the ice. The mother, who was feeding under the ice, pops up through the hole, climbs up on the ice, and begins to nurse her young.

On a rocky Arctic coast, a polar bear walks near a herd of walruses who are sleeping in the sun. One of the bulls wakes up, sees the white bear, and roars. The other walruses wake up and begin to snarl and groan. The walruses drag their bodies toward the water and scramble in.

31

When swimming, the sea lion seems to fly through the water. It pulls itself along with powerful strokes of its flippers.

Sea lions, seals, and walruses are classified as *pinnipeds*, or fin-footed animals. They are adapted to life in the sea. Their ancestors were bearlike animals that lived on land fifty to sixty million years ago.

All pinnipeds have shortened limbs. These are hardly more than hands and feet sticking out of the body. The limbs are webbed or finlike and adapted for swimming and diving.

Pinnipeds spend part of the time on land. Whales do not. Various species of pinnipeds gather on certain islands, on rocky and sandy beaches, or on ice floes to breed and raise their young. They sleep, rest, and molt, or shed their fur, on land.

Sea lions move well on land, but seals and walruses are awkward. Sea lions can jump from rock to rock. They also can turn their hind limbs forward and use them in walking.

*The seal swims by
beating the back part of
its body up and down.*

Sea lions are speedy swimmers who seem to fly through the water on their bellies or backs, twirling and making sharp turns. They leap out of the water and dive back in as dolphins do. Their bodies are torpedo-shaped, which reduces drag in the water. They can reach very high speeds in the water.

The sea lion swims with powerful downward and backward strokes of its forelimbs, or flippers. The flippers are actually long, webbed fingers. They provide the forelimbs with a broad surface area for pulling through the water. The hind limbs are held straight backward.

Seals and dolphins both move the rear part of their bodies up and down when they swim. A seal's webbed hind limbs work the way a whale's tail flukes work. Its forelimbs are of little use except for steering. On land, seals wriggle or hump along the way a caterpillar moves. They move surprisingly fast on land, snow, or ice. In Norway, a seal once traveled thirty-five miles over snow in one week.

The sea lion has small,
external ears. Its teeth,
like those of carnivores,
are adapted for eating
meat.

A sea lion's skull. The
canine fangs and sharp
cheek teeth are well
suited for seizing and
holding fish or squid.

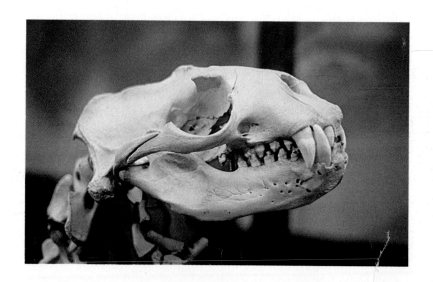

The teeth of pinnipeds, like those of most carnivores, are adapted for meat eating. Two canine fangs extend from the upper front part of the mouth. The cheek teeth, or molars, have sharp cusps (edges), which are less suited for chewing than for grabbing and holding prey. Sea lions and many seals prey on herring, salmon, cod, and other fish, as well as squid and octopus. The food is swallowed whole.

The California sea lion is the "trained seal" of circuses and shows. Sea lions can throw balls back and forth and balance them on their noses. The animals slide down slides and bark when their trainers reward them with fish or friendly pats.

California sea lions live in large numbers along the coast of northern California as well as in British Columbia, Japan, and the Galapagos Islands. A large bull is about seven and one-half feet long and weighs five hundred to six hundred pounds. Females weigh between two hundred and four hundred pounds and are shorter animals. Steller's sea lion, a species that lives along the Pacific coast from San Francisco to Alaska, is twice as large as the California sea lion. Sea lion fur is brown but appears black when wet.

The skull of a crab-eater seal. Its teeth are suited for straining tiny zooplankton from the sea.

During the breeding season, one bull usually keeps a harem of ten to twenty females. He mates with most of them. After a *gestation* of eleven to twelve months, the females give birth to single pups and nurse them on land.

When storms come, many pups die. The mothers try to carry the pups away from the waves by the scruff of the neck. When the female thinks that her pup is old enough to swim, she nudges it toward the water.

Sea lions and fur seals have small external ears and are called *eared seals.* Other seal species do not have external ears and are called *earless seals.*

Sea lions dive to depths of more than one hundred feet and can stay underwater for up to fifteen minutes. Many California sea lions live for fifteen to twenty years, but a few live to be thirty years old.

Like sea lions, seals are found along the coasts and near the islands of all cold-water oceans. The many species of seals include harbor seals, gray seals, northern fur seals, bearded seals, monk seals, harp seals, ringed seals, elephant seals, leopard seals, and crab-eating seals. Many millions of seals have been hunted and killed for their fur.

Many ringed seals actually live under solid ice floes. They use holes in the ice to breathe or to climb up on the ice to give birth to young. Ringed seals are often preyed on by polar bears.

The bull elephant seal has a long, trunklike nose. It is the largest member of the pinnipeds, weighing three and one-half to four tons.

The males of many mammal species normally have several mates. But the fur seal is known to have forty, fifty, or even one hundred of them. He keeps the largest harem of any mammal species. The bull fights any males who try to socialize with the females in his harem.

The harbor seal and most other seal species do not have external ears.

The large crab-eater seal lives in the coastal waters of the Antarctic Ocean. But it does not feed on crabs. Its teeth cannot crack open crabs and shellfish. Instead, like the baleen whale, it feeds mainly on swarms of tiny krill. The crab-eater seal swims into the swarm, opens its mouth, bites, and clenches its teeth. The seawater runs out. The food is retained and swallowed. There are between two million and five million crab-eater seals.

The harbor seal is another common seal. It lives in bays and harbors in the northern part of the world. Harbor seals spend more time in shallow waters and on sandy beaches than most seals do. They also swim into freshwater rivers and lakes. Herring, cod, and other coastal fishes are the main prey of harbor seals.

Harbor seal pups are born on remote, sandy beaches. They often howl when their mothers go off to seek food. These seals are easily tamed and breed successfully in captivity. They live long lives of thirty to thirty-seven years.

The walrus is a large, blubbery, fin-footed mammal. Its tusks are usually worn down or missing when the animal is kept in zoos.

Why Do Walruses Have Tusks?

Is there any animal more comical to look at than a walrus? It is a big, blubbery creature with a beard of bristly whiskers and long jutting tusks on a homely face. To the Vikings, who hunted whales and walruses more than a thousand years ago, the name *walrus* meant "whale horse."

At one time, walruses lived on the coasts of Holland and southern England. Walruses were also found all along the Atlantic coast from Newfoundland to Maine to Florida. But today, walruses are found only in the North Atlantic, North Pacific, and the waters off northern Siberia, Greenland, and the Arctic regions.

Walruses congregate in herds in shallow coastal waters and on rocky coasts and islands. They also gather on ice floes and icebergs.

A large bull between eleven and fourteen feet in length may weigh more than a ton. During the cold winter, the bull carries up to 900 pounds of blubber and may weigh 3,500 pounds. The cows, which are somewhat smaller, weigh between 1,600 and 1,800 pounds.

In man and many other mammals, the roots of the teeth close after the teeth have reached a certain size. Then all tooth growth stops. But the tusks of walruses remain open at the roots. These long teeth continue to grow throughout the animal's life. Both sexes have long tusks, which are very important in feeding. The tusks are chopping, digging, and hacking teeth.

When feeding, the walrus dives one hundred to two hundred feet to the ocean floor. At the bottom, it digs out clams, mussels, oysters, and other mollusks from the mud, sand, or gravel with its tusks. The walrus crushes the hard shells with its cheek teeth. It spits out the shells and swallows the soft parts inside.

Walruses also haul their bodies out of the water onto the ice floes with their tusks. They have been called "creatures that walk with their teeth" because they also use the tusks for dragging themselves along.

The typical walrus family consists of an old bull with one to three cows and a few young. The female's pregnancy, like that of most pinnipeds, is eleven to twelve months. The pups are usually born in April or May.

The mother never lets her pup stray out of sight. If a walrus from another family approaches the pup, the mother may attack and try to hack the other walrus with her tusks.

Many male walruses live in large "bachelor" herds, which stay away from the family groups.

If it gets the chance, a walrus will capture a seal. It grabs the seal with its webbed forelimb, hacks at it with its tusks to kill it, and feeds on the blubber.

40

The skull of a walrus with long tusks. Both sexes have tusks, which are used to dig oysters, clams, and other shellfish from the sea floor.

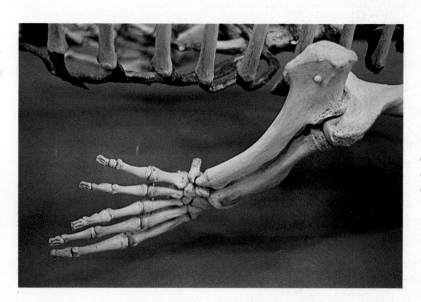

The forelimb of a walrus. The long fingers are covered with skin, creating a webbed hand or foot.

When a walrus dives, the web-footed hind limbs are last to follow.

Eskimos and other Arctic peoples hunt walruses. They eat walrus meat and use the skin for boats and dwellings, the oil for light and fuel, and the ivory tusks for tools and art objects. When tanned, the skin makes an excellent leather. The thicker parts of the skin have been used for centuries for making strong straps. Walruses have been known to capsize Eskimo hunters in their kayaks and drag them under the water.

When walruses are kept in captivity, they quickly become tame and friendly. They usually wear their tusks down by scraping them against the concrete walls and floors of their pools. In zoos, walruses cannot grub for mollusks. Keepers feed them a careful diet of clam meat and filleted (deboned) fish. Walruses sometimes amuse onlookers by squirting blasts of water at them.

The future of the marine mammals depends on well-balanced food chains in the sea, including an abundance and wide variety of plant and animal life. Sea lions, many seals, dolphins, and porpoises continue to breed in large numbers. But the future is in doubt for walruses, some seal species, sea otters, and many large baleen whales. Many nations must agree to protect the marine environments and restrict hunting in the sea. Otherwise, many wonderful creatures will be lost forever.

In zoos, the walrus is fed by keepers, and does not have to grub for its own food. A healthy walrus will live thirty to forty years.

Glossary (as the author used the words)

adapted	able to work and function in its environment
algae	tiny, microscopic plants that drift in the sea, producing oxygen and food for all other plant and animal life
aquatic	growing, feeding, or living in the water
baleen	whalebone; long, horny plates in the mouth of large whales used for straining krill from the sea
blowhole	whale's nostril
blubber	insulating layer of fat located under the skin of whales, dolphins, sea lions, seals, and walruses
carnivore	meat-eating animal
cetaceans	whales and other members of the whale family, including dolphins and porpoises
delphinids	members of the dolphin family: killer whales, dolphins, porpoises, and pilot whales
dorsal fin	fin located on the back of a whale or a fish
eared seals	sea lions and fur seals that have small, external ears
earless seals	seal species that do not have external ears
echolocation	ability of a whale to locate food and other objects by sending out sounds and having them bounce back like echoes
external	outside, on the body
flippers	forelimbs, or pectoral fins, of whales, dolphins, and sea lions
floe	low, flat mass of floating ice that forms in the sea
flukes	whale's broad, horizontal tail fin
gestation	pregnancy; period of time a mammal grows in its mother's womb, or uterus, before birth
herbivore	plant-eating animal
krill	shrimplike zooplankton that drift in huge swarms and are eaten by large whales and other marine animals
mammal	animal that nurses its young with milk secreted from its mammary glands
marine	relating to the sea or the ocean

organism	tiny animal with simple or complex organs
pectoral fins	forelimbs or flippers of whales or pinnipeds which are located near the breast
pinnipeds	fin-footed or web-footed marine mammals; seals, sea lions, and walruses as a family
plankton	all plant and animal life that drifts near the surface of the sea and is at the mercy of the currents
predator	animal that hunts, kills, and eats other animals to survive
pregnancy	gestation; period of time a mammal grows in its mother's womb, or uterus, before birth
prey	animals hunted, killed, and eaten by predators
species	group of animals with common characteristics
spy hopping	whale's ability to raise its body straight up out of the water and look far across the surface
zooplankton	krill and other tiny animals that drift in the sea, such as shrimp, crabs, shellfish, snails, water fleas, jellyfish, fish eggs, and larvae

INDEX

About the Author

Don Arthur Torgersen is an author, poet, editor, and producer. He was born in Chicago, attended Chicago public schools, and received his higher education at the University of Illinois, University of Hawaii, and University of Chicago. During the Korean War, he enlisted in the U.S. Navy and was engaged in naval communications and electronics. Mr. Torgersen has written and produced documentaries, educational filmstrips, anthologies, textbooks, children's stories, wildlife and animal behavior stories, and audiovisual programs for government and industry. He lives in a Chicago suburb with his wife, Kathleen, and three young sluggers named Scott, Dana, and Guy. His other activities include giving lectures and poetry readings, piano playing, enjoying opera and classical music, traveling, photography, mountain climbing, skiing, sailing, and managing a boys' baseball team. Mr. Torgersen has developed the Animal Safari Nature Library to introduce animal lovers and young naturalists to the wonderful animal kingdom, the basic terms and classifications in zoology, and the fascinating aspects of animal behavior.

About the Photographer

Lee Trail is a professional photographer and photo-journalist who lives in Champaign, Illinois. She was born in Chicago, attended the University of Chicago Lab School, and received her higher education at the University of Illinois. Widely traveled, Ms. Trail has done documentaries and educational photography in the United States, Canada, Europe, Africa, Central and South America, and the West Indies. She has also done commercial photography for advertising and industry. Her interest in animal photography began on field work studies for the University of Illinois Natural History Survey. When not on assignment, Ms. Trail is active in equestrian jumping competition, gourmet cooking, scuba diving, flying, and falconry.

DATE DUE

NOV 9		NOV 1 8 1998	
FEB 1 8 1979		FEB 12 2001	
SEP 2 2 1999			
OCT 1 1999			
NOV 5 1999			
DEC 8 1999			
JAN 2 6			
FEB 1 6 2000			
FEB 2 4 2000			
FEB 2 4 2000			
FEB 2 4 2000			
FEB 7 7 2000			
MAY 3 2000			

GAYLORD | | | PRINTED IN U.S.A.